Presented to:

_____

From:

_____

Date:

_____

USA
Activated Ministries
P.O. Box 462805
Escondido, CA 92046-2805
USA
Tel: 1-877-862-3228
E-mail: sales@actmin.org
www.activatedonline.com

EUROPE
Activated Europe
Bramingham Park Business Centre
Enterprise Way, Luton
LU3 4BU
United Kingdom
Tel: +44 (0) 845 8381384
E-mail: orders@activatedeurope.com
www.activatedeurope.com

SOUTH AFRICA
Big Thought Publications
PO Box 2509
Faerie Glen
Pretoria 0043
South Africa
Tel: 0861 888 918
E-mail: info@bigthought.co.za
www.bigthought.co.za

CANADA
Coloring the World Productions
P.O. Box 1034
135 West Beaver Creek Rd
Richmond Hill, ON
L4B 4R9
Canada
E-mail: activatedcanada@ica.net

PHILIPPINES
Activated Philippines
P.O. Box 1147
Antipolo City P.O.
1870 Antipolo City
Philippines
Tel: +63 2 9852540
E-mail: activatedpi@activated.org

WORLDWIDE
Hong Yuin Co., Ltd
*(A wholly owned subsidiary of
Aurora Production AG)*
9 Xingren Rd, Danshui District
New Taipei City
Taiwan
Tel: +886-2-26266725
E-mail: info@auroraproduction.com
Online shop: shop.auroraproduction.com

Selected by M. S. Fontaine

Creative director: Giselle LeFavre

Design by Yoko Matsuoka

Cover design by Laurent Mignot

ISBN: 978-3-03730-486-0

© 2012 Aurora Production AG, Switzerland

Printed in Taiwan. All rights reserved.

www.auroraproduction.com

FROM JESUS WITH LOVE

MY *Healing Touch*

Acknowledgements

All scripture quotations are taken from
the New King James Version®.

Copyright © 1982 by Thomas Nelson, Inc.
Used by permission. All rights reserved.

TABLE OF CONTENTS

INTRODUCTION

From the day we are born till the day we die, we are all susceptible to sickness and disease. As young children we instinctively look to and trust our parents to pull us through, but sooner or later we find that all their love, concern, and experience can take the healing process only so far. Then as we get older we learn to appreciate our body's amazing ability to overcome and recover from sickness, and we depend on that. But eventually we each find ourselves in a situation where that's not enough either. Who do we turn to for help then?—Doctors? God? Does God even want to get involved in our personal health problems? If so, what can we expect from Him, and what does He expect from us?

Healing is a very personal experience. Not only is each person different, but so is every illness and the surrounding circumstances. Moreover, healing usually involves both physical and spiritual factors. Many people who seek healing focus on the physical while ignoring the spiritual, and a few become so focused on the spiritual that they forget to correct the physical causes. How do we find the proper balance?

Some of the spiritual principles involved are basic and universal—believing that divine intervention is possible, finding God's purpose in allowing the illness, doing whatever He may require in each particular situation, claiming His promises, and continuing to trust Him even when the answer isn't immediate or what we expect. But God also takes other factors into consideration, such as the person's spiritual maturity and knowledge of His ways.

Many people don't realize that from God's viewpoint, healing of the body is not always the primary or only goal. Often the greater need is for healing of the spirit. To accomplish that, He sometimes puts us in a position where He can get through to us better on the spiritual level. Physical afflictions are one of the most effective means He has of doing that, as they force us to stop long enough to listen to what He has to say.

Yet another factor is that our own spirits aren't the only ones involved. The Bible tells us that a fierce, continual battle is taking place in the unseen spiritual realm that surrounds us. It's a battle of good against evil for influence over our hearts and minds, which in turn control our actions and destinies. As God and His heavenly forces war against the Devil and his demons, the battle spills over into our physical realm and involves us. "We do not wrestle against flesh and blood, but against principalities, against powers, against the rulers of the darkness of this age, against spiritual hosts of wickedness in the heavenly places."[1] One way that the Devil and his demons attack us is through our health, so it's important that we keep our spiritual defenses strong in order to help ward off sickness, and also that we pray about possible spiritual causes when we do get sick.

Even if you try to approach healing from a purely physical angle, there is no black-and-white formula that applies in every case. For example, the question of whether or not to seek professional

---

1. Ephesians 6:12

help in the form of doctors, medicines, treatments, therapies, or other physical means is nearly always a multi-faceted one, and again every case is different. A course of action that may be right in one case may be totally wrong in another. This is true of special diets, medicines, surgery, radiology, chemotherapy, chiropractic, or any other procedure or treatment. The world is filled with books telling people what to do or not do to get healed. Some approaches sometimes work and sometimes don't. Many contradict one another. Who's to say which approach would be best in your case? Which expert will you trust?

Jesus is the Great Physician. He knows more about your body and how to fix it than all the other doctors put together. Not only that, but He also understands and is concerned about the whole person—body, mind, and spirit. He sometimes uses doctors and treatments as His instruments to facilitate healing, but He's the only one who has real healing power. No healing is possible without His involvement at some level, so why not involve Him in every case, from the beginning, and at every level? He would like nothing better, as He explains on the following pages.

So when you need healing, put yourself first and foremost in His loving hands. If He chooses to heal you through supernatural means alone, that's within His power. If He chooses to enlist the help of doctors, He wants to head the team. If He chooses to heal you instantly, that's within His power too. If He chooses to let you suffer physically for a while so your spirit can be strengthened, that's His prerogative and He does so in love. If He chooses to heal you through death—by taking you to heaven, where there is no more sickness, sorrow, or suffering—this is also part of His great unfailing love.

In any case, His goal is not temporary physical healing today so you can get sick again tomorrow. He could fix you a million times and your mortal body would just keep breaking till its dying day. His goal is to help you be as happy, healthy, and fulfilled as possible in this life, while preparing you for the next. He has a design for your life, and working with you through sickness is one way He has of helping you conform to His design. More than anything, He wants you to be all you can be.

The following messages from Jesus don't contain everything He has to say to you about healing in general, or cover every situation you will ever face. There's a lot more where this came from! Jesus wants to open a personal hotline between you and Him so He can give you personal answers to your questions and problems. You, too, can hear directly from Jesus. He will speak to anyone who believes in Him, sincerely asks Him to speak, and then accepts by faith that what they "hear" in their mind is truly Him speaking. Receiving and following His guidance is the single most important step towards good health.

Open your life and heart to receive His healing touch.

CHAPTER 1

GETTING STARTED

I love you—yes, you!

My love for you is everlasting. My love for you is unstoppable. My love for you reaches up to the highest star and down to the depths of the deepest sea. My love for you is always. It's now, and it's forever. It's alive, vibrant. I want you to experience My love in full measure so your faith can blossom, so you will believe that I can and want to meet your every need. I died for you, and now I live for you. I will do *anything* for you!

I long to comfort, to soothe, and to pour on you My healing balm, to ease your worries, your fears, your frustrations, and to dry your every tear. My love is reaching out to you right now. I will fill your heart to overflowing with My love. You have only to ask. Anywhere, any time, every minute of the day or night I'll be there to prove My love in some way. When you feel confusion, I will give you peace. When you feel fearful, I will comfort your heart. When you're besieged by doubts, I will give you faith. When you feel stressed, I will bring relief. When you feel lost and alone, I'm right there. When all seems dark and stormy, I will be your shining light. In big ways and small ways, I'm always there, ready, willing, and waiting to shower you with love. I will never let you down, and that's a promise.

Ever-present help

I don't want you to look at this sickness as something that I stand back and watch you go through—you there and Me here. It's never been like that, really, and I certainly don't want it to be like that now.

My heart breaks to see you in pain—not only the physical pain, but also the mental and spiritual attacks that come with it, the thoughts of helplessness and hopelessness. Please believe that I never allow anything to happen to you who love Me that's not in some way for your good. Hang on to that promise.

I know it hurts, and I feel for you. I'm right here by your side. No, I'm not even that distant; I surround you, covering all the sore spots, soothing as only I can, and I won't leave you for an instant.

In times of pain, I will bring sweet relief. In times of distress, I will be your comforter. In times of doubt, I will fan your spark of faith. In your darkest hour, I will be your guiding light. In times of torment, I will be your safe haven. In times of emptiness, I will be your all in all.

Prayer's healing power

The human body is vulnerable to sickness and disease. That's part of the human condition. There are some precautions you can take to help maintain good health, and some remedies you can use to facilitate the natural healing process, but none of these are cure-alls, none of them get permanent results, and sometimes they simply aren't enough. Sometimes you need something more—*spiritual* help. That help is Mine to freely give, and I make it available to you through prayer. Your prayers for healing set in motion My spiritual power, which can then go to work on fixing your physical body.

You can't see electricity, but you know it exists because you can see its effects. You flip the switch and the light comes on or the appliance does what it was made to do, and your life is better for it. Well, prayer is just as real, but far more wonderful. It's the means for bringing heavenly spiritual power to your earthly plane—power that can do all sorts of marvelous things, including heal your body when needed.

But just as all the electricity in the world won't do you a bit of good unless you tap into it, all that heavenly power to heal won't do you a bit of good unless you avail yourself of it. Flip the switch, connect with Me, and My infinite resources are at your command.

I CAN HEAL ANYTHING

I told My first followers, "All authority has been given to Me in heaven and on earth" and "whatever you ask in My name, that I will do for you."[1] Those promises have inspired millions concerning My ability to answer prayer. Now all that power is waiting for *you* and can be activated through your prayers. There is absolutely no limit to what I can do!

I can heal anything. I can even restore life and health to someone who has died! I raised people from the dead while I trod the dusty roads of Palestine two thousand years ago, and My power has not diminished since. If I could do that, surely I can heal whatever's wrong with you!

I can do the impossible, and I delight in difficult cases. I can do anything you ask of Me, if you believe. I want to prove that to you. I can bring full health and strength to your weakened body. I can bring perfect peace and rest to your troubled mind. I can bring joy and light to your aching heart.

My healing power is greater than any medicine or treatment, so call on Me and I will pour My healing balm upon you, according to your request and according to your faith. Expect a miracle!

---

1. Matthew 28:18; John 14:13

Our contract

How do you receive healing?—The same way you receive anything else from Me: You just have to ask, believe My promises, do your part, and trust that I'll answer in the way that I know is best for you.

My Word[1] is like a contract between you and Me that contains many specific promises to you personally, including promises that I can and will heal you in answer to prayer. As with any contract, there are certain terms that both parties must meet, but if you'll study this contract

I think you'll agree that I've made it as easy for you as I possibly could. All I ask is that you meet a few basic conditions, such as humbly admitting your need, asking for My help, and having your heart right with Me and others.

In our contract I've also reserved the right to do what's best for you and others involved, even if that means not answering your prayer exactly how or when you asked Me to. You usually assume that what you want is what's best, but only I

know what's *truly* best. You usually want immediate results, but I often want to accomplish other things first, so that the overall result will be even greater. So when you ask for healing, include in your prayer, "Do what *You* know is best." If the time and other conditions are right, I will heal you. But if you don't see the answer right away, don't doubt and despair. I'm just waiting till I can give you the best.

Once you have done your part, you can point to My promises,[2] hold Me to them, and be assured that I will always honor our contract. I'm true to My word!

---

1. God's Word includes the Bible and other divinely inspired writings. It can also include messages received from God's Spirit in prophecy.

2. You'll find a list of some of the many promises in the Bible about healing on page 57 of this book.

More power to you

Prayer has great power, and asking others to pray with you, "united prayer," has even more. I told My first disciples, "If two of you agree on earth concerning anything that they ask, it will be done for them by My Father in heaven."[1]

The apostle James also instructed the first Christians, "Is anyone among you sick? Let him call for the elders of the church, and let them pray over him, anointing him with oil in the name of the Lord. And the prayer of faith will save the sick, and the Lord will raise him up."[2] "Elders of the church" can be anyone who believes in My power to heal. It helps if you're together when you pray because hearing one another's prayers encourages your faith, but I still consider it "united prayer" when you unite in purpose and faith, wherever you each may be.

If circumstances prevent you from asking anyone else to pray for you, I will still hear and answer your prayer. The "anointing with oil" is symbolic of My healing balm, which you're asking Me to pour upon you. The oil (and it can be something as simple as cooking oil) doesn't heal, but is a demonstration of your faith in My power.

The bottom line: Ask others to pray for you if you can, and demonstrate your faith however you can, but I'm not bound by ceremony. Do what you can, and "the prayer of faith will save the sick."

---

1. Matthew 18:19
2. James 5:14–15

CHAPTER 2

THE GREAT PHYSICIAN

I'VE BEEN THERE

I can talk on the subject of sickness, because I've been there. I know what it's like to be sick—the hardship, the pain, the suffering—because when I came to earth as a man, I went through all the things that you experience, including sickness and injury. As the Son of God, I had power to work great miracles; I healed multitudes and even brought some back to life. I could just as easily have healed Myself whenever I got sick. But I didn't, as I needed to experience all the trials and temptations you do.[1] I suffered on earth that I might have the heart of both God and man, to understand the depths of your need and then to fill that need.

I also suffered ill health for much the same reasons that you do—to help Me appreciate the good health I had most of the time, to help Me to learn patience, to give Me more time alone with My Father in quietness and stillness to think and pray about things, and to cause Me to love Him all the more when He healed Me.

I know what it's like to live with pain, and I know what it's like to feel alone in that suffering. I went through all that for you, so you would never have to be alone in your suffering, and you're not. I'm here to love and comfort and, when the time is right, make whole.

---

1. Hebrews 4:15

Healing is a gift

You don't get healed by trying to be perfect, any more than you can obtain salvation and get to heaven that way. You can't get saved until you realize that only I could pay the price for your salvation, and it's not until you realize that you need Me for healing that I'm able to step in and do the miracle. "By grace you are saved through faith,"[1] and by grace you are healed through faith.

Healing is a gift, but it's also a reward in a sense. It is the reward of faith. How much faith it takes depends on the person and situation. For some, such as those who do not yet know Me in a real and personal way, I make the conditions as easy as possible: only that they believe and ask. Sometimes I even heal them in response to other people's prayers and faith. But I expect more from those who know Me, and know how I want them to live their lives: I expect them to demonstrate their faith by putting that knowledge into practice.

Don't try to work up your healing or worry that you aren't good enough. Of course you're not good enough—no one is. That's why it has to be a gift. Just humbly admit that you need it, believe that it's waiting for you in My outstretched hand, accept it by faith, and thank Me for it.

---

1. Ephesians 2:8

I SUFFERED FOR YOUR HEALING

I died for you so you could have eternal life, but before My crucifixion I also suffered a cruel scourging at the hands of ungodly men so the scripture would be fulfilled, "By His stripes we are healed."[1]

I didn't have to go through all of that—the beating and whipping and mockery—for your salvation; I only had to die on the cross. But I was willing to also go through all that pain and suffering and humiliation because I cared about your pain and suffering. I felt for you, and I didn't want you to have to go through one moment of illness or pain if I could spare you that. I wanted to give you a way out, and I did. I gave My body for yours, so I can now offer you the gift of healing as well as the gift of salvation.

This gift of healing is so great and so universally needed that I made it a part of the only ceremony I asked My first disciples to observe—the ceremony that has come to be called Communion. The Communion bread symbolizes My body, which was broken for your healing. Every time you partake of the Communion bread, you are remembering My sacrifice and claiming the promise attached to it as your own.

Come to Me when you are sick and afflicted. Receive My healing and be made whole, for healing is one of the manifestations of My love for you.

---

1. Isaiah 53:5

CHAPTER 3

SICKNESS AS
I SEE IT

The big picture

I see the long-range plan, the big picture. I see into eternity. The natural man sees only the moment, especially when he's wracked with pain and problems. But I want to help you look beyond the moment, beyond the scope of the natural man, into the realm of the spirit, which is where I work.

To the natural man, sickness is a setback; to you and Me, it will be an opportunity to draw closer than we could under other circumstances. To the natural man's way of thinking, every illness must surely be a punishment from an angry, displeased God; to us, it will be another chance for Me to prove and for you to feel My unfailing love for you. To the natural man, this is an awful burden; to us, it will be a load that's light because we'll bear it together. To the natural man, things like this are practically the end of the world—his world; for us, it will be a gateway to a better world—the spiritual realm where your spirit can grow and progress.

Through illness and other problems, I prepare your spirit for the future—not only for your future in this life, but also for your eternal future. In the grand scope of things, your present suffering can't be compared to the eternal payoff. When you get up here and the whole spectrum of life and reality is revealed to you, you'll be glad that you went through what you did.

"Is God punishing me?"

Sometimes people bring illness or injury on themselves through their own foolishness, carelessness, or disregard for natural or spiritual laws. In those cases, the afflictions *are* a punishment of sorts. But even then, it's punishment with a purpose: to help the person learn through experiencing the consequences of their bad choices.

Often, however, the affliction isn't a punishment at all; it's My way of bringing about some greater good in your life.

The Devil, "the accuser," as the Bible calls him, is always right there to remind you why you don't deserve good health or My healing touch or any of My other blessings. He will try to convince you that

it's only fair that you suffer for your mistakes and shortcomings. That's the Devil's justice—but it's not My way.

Even if you did bring the affliction on yourself, even if there is something that I'm trying to teach you through it, I always give hope, peace, and promise of blessing the instant you turn to Me, ask forgiveness, and determine to make wiser and healthier choices. That's My promise to you! Hang on to that promise, and don't let the Devil drag you down with discouragement. Bring your questions to Me, tell Me your fears, and let Me gently wipe away every trace of condemnation. I will make it right, all right. All you have to do is turn to Me.

"Why me?"

People often question why I allow some to suffer more serious or frequent health problems than others. Is it because I think some "deserve" it more? If that's the case, why do "good" people seem to have more than their share of illnesses? Isn't that a bit unfair? And when it's they who seem to have more than their share, the real question becomes, "Why me?" Those are all valid questions. Here's the short answer:

I work differently in each person's life, because people are different. Their faith is different, their relationship with Me is different, and the lessons they need to learn at any given time are different. I have a special plan for your life too. It's a good plan and all for your good, even though it may not always seem so to you. I don't push My plan on you—I'm not out to control you or prove who's boss—but I do try to steer you in the right direction.

I do so out of love, to help you, but even so, learning qualities such as wisdom, love, compassion, understanding, humility, and selflessness is sometimes a difficult and painful process, especially when I use sickness as a catalyst.

Sometimes, however, a particular sickness isn't part of My plan, nor is it due to any fault of yours. Rather, the enemy of your soul, the Devil, is trying to bring you down. He will do anything he can to come between you and Me, make right living difficult, and generally interfere with your happiness, and sickness is one of his favorite tools.

Whatever the cause, when I allow you to get sick or suffer injury, I can cause it to benefit you in some way. Trust in that promise, and you will find that the good always outweighs the bad.

Spiritual tune-up

Often I use afflictions in the lives of My children as a chance for Me to give them a spiritual tune-up. Consider these benefits:

- It slows you down. You're not able to keep going "business as usual"—which often means too busy for Me.
- Then once you've slowed down and I have your attention, you're in a position to reexamine your life. You take stock of your values and priorities.
- It brings humility, because it reminds you of how weak you are. And when you need to ask for help and prayer from others, that can be humbling too.
- You become more attuned to My Spirit and more open to whatever I may want to teach you through it.

- It gives you a greater appreciation for the good health you normally have, and greater compassion for others who are weak.
- It gets you to change bad habits that may have contributed to your getting sick.
- It brings out the best in others as they love and care for those who are weak. It strengthens the bonds of love between family and friends.
- It gets everyone praying more, which is always a good thing.

So you see, there are *many* benefits—and those aren't even all of them!

Chapter 4

That Thing Called Faith

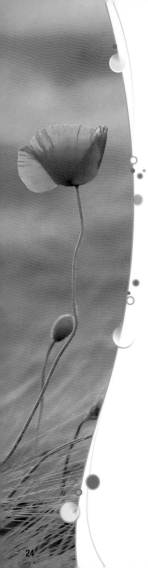

THE SOURCE OF FAITH

When you're sick, if you're ruled by your feelings, you're sunk! Your body feels miserable, and your spirit will soon follow if you're not careful. And if you go by the "facts"—the state of things as they appear in the physical realm—that can get you down just as bad. The only thing that can buoy your spirit is faith, and the only source of faith in Me is My Word.

Faith comes from studying My Word—not just reading it casually, but really thinking about what it means and how it applies to you. That's how faith is born. But to become strong and mature, faith needs to be put to use. It needs to be stretched and strengthened, and that's something that you can and should do by taking action on what My Word says.

Faith goes beyond merely believing. You can believe something in theory, but it doesn't do you any good until you put it to use. As you put My promises to the test and watch Me honor them, you will know beyond a shadow of a doubt that they're true. Being a doer of the Word will help you build the rock-solid foundation you need when your faith gets tested.[1]

Faith doesn't just happen. You have to put some effort into acquiring it. Read the Word, memorize the Word, listen to the Word, talk about the Word, and above all *live* the Word.

---

1. James 1:22–25

Wishful thinking?
—Or expectancy?

A lot of people pray to be healed or for this or that, and then are disappointed when I don't answer. Why don't I answer? Often it's because the people praying don't really expect Me to. Their prayers are really no more than wishes—vague, wistful, wouldn't-it-be-nice thoughts. Wishes aren't the same as prayers because they lack the all-important element of faith, which is demonstrated by expectancy.

Having faith for healing means that you not only *believe* that I can heal you and that it's My will, but you *expect* Me to. And because you expect results, you can be very definite and firm in your prayer. You can point to the promises in My Word that say I *can* and *want to* and *will* heal, count it a done deal, and thank Me for the miracle, even before you see it.

The main thing that limits My power coming through is the level of your faith, and that's measured by your expectancy— what you're sure I'm going to do in response to your prayers. It pleases Me greatly when you boldly make your request, because that shows that you not only realize you need My help, but also that you're confident that I can and will work on your behalf. I reward full-of-faith prayers because they show that you're depending on Me for your healing, and that you believe I *will* do the miracle for you.

Faith is the victory!

Faith guarantees victory!—Faith in Me, faith in My Word, faith in My promises in spite of how you feel, in spite of the circumstances, in spite of what your body may be telling you, in spite of obstacles or setbacks or disappointments or anything else. Faith is the deciding factor.

As you fill up on My promises and focus on My power that's behind them, I'll give you the faith you need. And as you exercise your faith, you'll feel Me living and working in you in ways you never even imagined before. Faith instantly summons My miracle-working power.

To think that I expect you to be always positive and full of faith when you're in the middle of a serious illness may seem like I'm expecting too much, but just take it one moment at a time. The smallest praise, the briefest prayer from the heart, or simply calling My name may be all you can muster, but that's enough. That's putting your faith into action, and that's what counts.

Faith is the victory, but it's not a once-and-for-all victory. You will undoubtedly face more battles in the future—as everyone does till their dying day—but there is no battle, no illness or other problem, that faith won't conquer. So don't worry about whether or not you'll have enough faith for the *next* test—just approach this one in faith, and take each one as it comes. Faith will prevail every time!

CHAPTER 5

DOING YOUR PART

An ounce of prevention

I have the power to heal you, but generally I'd rather help you stay healthy. Prevention is better than cure.

When you usually enjoy good health, you can sometimes take it for granted and get slack with the things you know you should do, like getting enough sleep, eating properly, drinking enough water, getting good exercise, and avoiding stress. When special circumstances necessitate, I can override the natural laws that govern your body and health, but I can't do so indefinitely.

If you're not taking care of yourself physically—or similarly, if you're not taking good care of your spiritual health by spending time with Me—then I sometimes use sickness to get you back on the straight and narrow. I don't do this as a punishment, but for your own good.

One key to good health that many people overlook is to pray for My protection and blessing. Through prayer, I'm able to shield you from germs or other outside factors that threaten your health. But just as "faith without works is dead,"[1] praying for good health is not enough. For Me to do My part, you must also do yours. Listen to your body, and listen to Me. Do your part, and I will do the rest.

1. James 2:26

A MEETING OF WILLS

Sometimes all it takes to get healed is a single, simple prayer—you pray, I answer, it's done. But other times even fervent and repeated prayers don't bring the desired results. What's wrong? Often it's that your will—what you want done—is out of sync with My will—what I know is best for you in this situation. There needs to be a meeting of wills, and there are really only two options for getting there, which I'll call Plan A and Plan B.

In Plan B, I compromise My will to conform to yours. That's within the realm of possibility, and I've done it before. If you insist on Plan B, however, you could be frustrated and disappointed. For one thing, you won't be able to pray in full faith if you know or suspect that you're at cross-purposes with Me. But worse, if I were to go along with your plan it would be only My second best. Like the Israelites who insisted on having it their way in the wilderness, you might get what you asked for, but along with it leanness to your soul.[1]

In Plan A, you sign your will over to Me and pray, "Not my will, but Yours be done." That takes real faith, especially when you don't know what My will is, but that's the only way you can be sure of getting My best. I definitely recommend Plan A.

_____

1. Psalm 106:15

Work with Me

To get the best results when praying for healing or anything else, don't just leave a "voice mail" message telling Me what you would like done. Stay on the line and I'll tell you what you can do to help speed the answer or make it more complete. I can give you counsel tailored to your situation.[1] For example, I might want you to claim miraculous healing because I know the sickness doesn't have to run its natural course. Or maybe there's something you need to do first, such as strengthening your faith through reading My Word, or getting your heart right with Me or others, or asking others to pray for you. Or I may be waiting for you to get more stirred up in spirit and to "fight the good fight of

faith"[2] by claiming My promises. Or there may be something that you need to do in the physical, such as changing your diet or getting more rest. Or I may be trying to get through to you about something that doesn't seem to have anything to do with the sickness, but this was the only way I could get your attention. I could have any of a number of things to tell you, but you'll probably never find out what they are unless you ask Me.

Half of the solution is in coming to Me, getting My counsel, and following through on it. Then, no matter what direction your sickness may take, you'll know you've done your part, and that will make it much easier to trust Me to do Mine. Knowing that you

have heard directly and specifically from Me about the illness will also give you more faith to *do* whatever is needed to overcome it.

No one can comfort and encourage you like I can! One of the quickest, simplest, and surest ways to get that comfort is to ask Me to speak to you heart to heart. When you connect with Me, I can personally give you words of love, comfort, and encouragement—special treasures of the spirit that you wouldn't gain any other way.

Even when you feel too weak to speak to Me, you can still hear My voice in your heart. You can always lift your heart to Me and be comforted by My words. Just point your spiritual antenna toward Me, ask Me to speak, and I will. Then lie back in My arms, hear My whispers in your heart, and let Me transport you in spirit out of this world of pain to be with Me in heavenly places. You can do it anytime, anywhere.

If you're not used to hearing Me speak to you, it may take a little practice, but if you believe and put forth the effort, I will help you learn to distinguish between your own thoughts and My voice so you can receive all that I have for you. Ask, listen, believe, and you will receive.

---

1. For more information about how to receive personal advice from Jesus, read *Hearing from Heaven*, available from Aurora Production.

2. 1 Timothy 6:12

Why praise?

It's a law of both the natural and spiritual realms that when you dwell on the good, then good surrounds you. When you think positive thoughts, speak positive words, and take positive action, you feel better and things generally work out better. Praising Me accelerates that positive cycle because it not only helps you to think on the good, but it moves you out of the physical realm, with all of its limitations, into the spiritual realm, where all things are possible.

When you're fighting a serious illness, it's easy to give in to feelings of discouragement or even despair. But if you determine to praise Me instead, if you start praising even when you don't feel like it, soon you will feel like it. Praising Me reminds you that I'm in control and will work everything out for your good.

When you praise Me, it strengthens our connection. That enables Me to speak to you more clearly so I can help put things in perspective. Praise puts you on My wavelength. It opens a channel in the spirit through which I can pour My blessings upon you.

Praising Me reminds you that only I am capable of solving your problems. Your praises prove to Me that you're depending on Me, that you're letting go of your own works and depending on My power to work the needed miracle.

Praise pleases Me and moves Me to work on your behalf, but it also motivates

you, encourages you, and causes you to see beyond your request and present circumstances, to focus instead on the fulfillment, and that's a key to receiving answers to your prayers.

Praise brings so much of My Spirit and so many of the fruits of My Spirit[1] into your life.

When you take a positive approach to illness—or any problem, for that matter—and express that in the form of praise to Me, you're manifesting faith in Me. That combination of faith and praise gives you an extra dose of grace and power to see you through the difficulty. In the case of illness, steps of faith carry you down the road to healing. As you praise Me, even if all you can do is whisper the words or say them in your heart, you will begin feeling My comfort and love. When you praise Me, your spirit is surrounded with supernatural power. And as you continue praising, I ease the pain and I bring relief and sweet rest.

Focus on the good, no matter how bad the situation seems to be. Praise Me for the things I have done for you in the past. Praise Me for the good health you normally have. Praise Me that your sickness isn't worse. Praise Me for the good that you can imagine Me accomplishing through this. Once you start praising Me more, you'll realize how much there is to praise Me about. Praise will turn your times of sickness into times of triumph.

1. Galatians 5:22–23

Staying healed

I never allow you to get sick without a reason, so when you get sick, one of the first things you should do is ask Me why. Doing what you can to correct the problem is often an important step toward getting healed, but it's an even more important factor in *staying* healed.

Just as there is always a reason for sickness, there are always intended benefits. These can be physical—immunity to a one-time disease, or getting rid of an unhealthy habit, for example—or they can be spiritual. The spiritual benefits are often even greater than the physical ones if you pray and hear from Me about them. Maybe I'm trying to teach you to be more prayerful, or to spend more time with Me and My Word, or to change one or more of your other spiritual habits. But if you just suffer through your sickness without asking Me what's going on and why, you can miss the point, miss the benefit, and set yourself up for a relapse or recurrence of the sickness and another chance to learn what you could have learned the first time around.

This is actually part of My purpose for the time of recuperation that follows most sickness—to give you time to pray about the lessons and commit yourself to making whatever changes might be needed, before you're caught up again in your routine and old habits. Don't let this chance pass you by.

The stand of faith

I love it when you come to Me with a specific promise—"Ask, and it will be given,"[1] for example—and put Me on the spot by asking Me to fulfill it. I love it even more when, after having done that, you exhibit confidence that I'm going to do what I said I would, even when I don't do it right away. Sometimes I like to strengthen your faith by *not* answering your prayer right away, or not answering it in the way you expect. I like to see you trusting that I know what I'm doing and won't fail you, no matter how hard or long the wait.

Have you read in the Bible about Shadrach, Meshach, and Abednego, how they were forced to choose whether to bow to an image and live, or stay true to God and be burned alive? They answered the king, "Our God whom we serve is able to deliver us from the burning fiery furnace, and He will deliver us. But if not…"[2] They were willing to die trusting. That's the stand of faith! Not only did I honor their stand by helping them come through the fire without so much as a singed hair, but I was *with* them in the fire. King Nebuchadnezzar witnessed four people in the fire, not three, and said that the fourth was like the Son of God."[3]

Stand fast on My promises. I will be there for you too.

_____

1. Matthew 7:7
2. Daniel 3:17–18
3. Daniel 3:25

Taking stock

Before you can say, "I have done what I could, now I'm going to trust God and hold Him to His promises for however long it takes until I'm healed"—before you take that kind of stand, you need to know that you have truly done all that you can and that whatever is preventing Me from healing you in answer to your prayer is truly beyond your control, not due to some neglect or oversight on your part. You should ask yourself questions like:

- Have I prayed about what Jesus may be trying to teach me through this, and about what He may be expecting of me before He can answer my prayer and heal me?
- Have I received Jesus' assurance that our wills are in agreement—that my desire to be healed speedily and completely is in line with His plan for me—or am I at least willing to leave my life in His hands, trusting that He is in control and knows what's the best outcome for me, even if it's not what I'm personally hoping for?

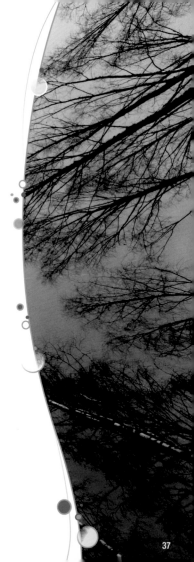

- Have I held a spiritual housecleaning by examining my heart and asking Jesus to deliver me from any unconfessed sins—bitterness, pride, criticalness, jealousy, or any other spiritual blockages that could be keeping me from receiving His full blessing?
- Have I strengthened my faith for healing through reading, meditating on, and applying the Word?
- Have I committed at least one of God's promises of healing to memory, and do I truly believe that He's able to do what He says He will do?
- Have my prayers been in faith, definite, and specific?
- Have I asked others to pray for me?

If you haven't done these things, then chances are you haven't done all that you can. There might be something missing on your part, something more that you can do. But if you have, you can take the stand of faith, trusting that I will heal you in My time and My way.

CHAPTER 6

HELPING HANDS

"According to Your Faith…"

In a sense, *all* healing is "faith healing." When you need healing, how you choose to try to go about it and whom you turn to for help takes faith in any case—faith in doctors and medicines, faith in Me alone, or faith that I will work through doctors and medicines to bring about the healing you need. Where does your faith lie? "According to your faith let it be to you."[1]

I can reach down in an instant and heal you with no help from anyone else if that's what you have faith for, if that's what you

expect Me to do, and if that's also My will for you in that situation. Or you can put your faith in others and their knowledge, skills, and remedies—but putting faith in fallible man can be risky. A much better approach is to pray that the doctors and medicines will be My instruments to bring about healing.

Whether you decide to trust Me to heal you without any help from doctors, or to consult a doctor to find out what's wrong so you can pray more effectively, or to trust

---

1. Matthew 9:29

39

Me to work through doctors in the healing process, the decision is yours. I can help you make the right decision, though, if you will look to Me for guidance.

Finding what's best in such an important matter as a serious illness is seldom a one-prayer-and-you're-done deal. You may have a very definite leading as to where to start—whether it's to trust Me to heal you through natural or supernatural means, or to seek medical help—but you should also pray for My guidance and a confirmation of My will each step of the way, especially before making major decisions. Doctors have their opinions and you have your preferences, but only I know what's best—and I'm *always* here to help "according to your faith."

A winning combination

If I have led you to seek medical help, I can also lead you to wise, competent doctors, so pray for that.

There's only so much that doctors can do, but I can step in and help them. I can enhance their skills, increase their knowledge, remind them of things they may have forgotten, and give them wisdom that's beyond their know-how and experience—*if* you pray for them.

I can work through anyone, but it's easiest for Me to work through those who have faith, spiritual people who believe in prayer, who realize that they aren't sufficient in themselves and so are more open to divine guidance and assistance. Pray for Me to lead you to such doctors. You will have more faith that we can work well as a team if you know that they're already in touch with Me, or at least open to you praying for them.

You should pray before and after every consultation or treatment. Pray that your doctors will be sensitive to My Spirit. Pray for Me to lead both you and the doctors in knowing what questions to ask, as well as for My wisdom as they diagnose the situation. Pray about possible courses of action, that they will help you make the best choices. As you pray, I will give your doctors and their staff wisdom and enhanced skill, so that they give you the best treatment possible—and you deserve the best, because you're My beloved child.

CHAPTER 7

TOUGH CASES

What if…?

What if you pray and nothing happens, or what if you're only healed for a little while? What's not right? Am I being unfair or making a mistake if I don't answer the way you'd like Me to, when you want Me to?—No. Whatever I do, I do it in love, and I don't make mistakes. Does it mean that you've failed or displeased Me or lack sufficient faith?—Not necessarily.

There are certain things that you must do before you can expect Me to heal you, not the least of which is to pray—and that doesn't necessarily mean to pray once and be done with it. You may need to keep praying, trusting, and waiting. For any of

a number of reasons, it takes Me longer to answer some prayers than others, and some I may never answer in the way you're asking. If you can trust Me for the outcome rather than insist that I heal you on your terms, if you're willing to put your life in My hands and leave it there, that's great faith.

If I don't heal, you can be sure that it is for a good reason, so put your life in My strong and caring hands. Then you can know that whatever happens will be what I want to happen because I know that's best in the long run and according to My perfect plan for your life.

Why all healing isn't instant

Not only can I heal anything, but I can do so instantly. If I could do it for the people you read about in the Gospels, I could heal everyone else at their first prayer as well, but in most cases I don't. Why?— Because I have something even better in mind.

To most people's way of thinking, instant, complete healing is the best kind—the ultimate in miracles of healing. Because instant healing is so spectacular, they think it's the result of spectacular faith. Well, they're wrong on both counts. Instant healing is a wonderful manifestation of My power, but it isn't necessarily the ultimate because it doesn't always benefit the person as much as another form of healing might, nor does it necessarily require as much faith. Instant healing only requires a one-time manifestation of faith, but other forms of healing require even greater faith—step-by-step faith, faith that's tested to the limits, faith that keeps trusting even when everything looks bleak. That, to Me, is far more spectacular.

Sometimes it's an even greater testimony to your faith when everything *doesn't* turn out as you wanted or expected—even though you prayed and did everything else you were supposed to— and you still trust Me. The longer the wait, the greater the test and the greater the faith, *if* you continue to stand on My promises and fight in prayer for your healing, trusting Me moment by moment that in My time and way I will answer.

LOVE AWAITS

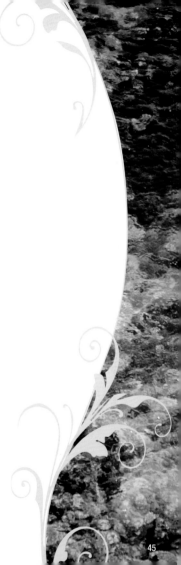

When the darkness closes in so tight that it seems to crowd out My presence, I'm still right here. In your darkest, most desperate moments, I never leave your side.

At the end of this long, dark corridor is the door to eternal life and love and joy such as you have never imagined in your wildest dreams. Life on earth is but a pale shadow of the next.—Merely a vapor, a brief preparation for the reality of life as you will soon experience it in My heavenly realm.

You're coming to your reward and the wonderment of seeing Me face to face, but still it's a struggle sometimes. Your mind is of this world and tries to hold on to the things of this world, while your spirit longs to be freed from the confines of its earthly shell. If only you knew how I look forward to the moment when I will hold you in My embrace, every part of you would feel the same way.

Soon you will doff the garment of your present body like an old, well-used garment, and enter into a realm where you shall never know sickness or pain or sorrow. I wait for the perfect moment. Until then, trust Me that I will not allow you to suffer one iota more or be tested one moment longer than I know you can bear. Here, take My hand. I will lead you through this dark tunnel toward the light.

Fight to the Finish

If you find yourself facing a serious long-term health problem that might even take your life, don't immediately say, "What's the use? I'm probably going to die anyway," and give up. If you can stay positive and trust Me no matter what—whether it's My will to help you beat the odds, or to bring you home to heaven—that's the kind of faith that pleases Me most! I couldn't be prouder of you than when you refuse to lose faith, when you refuse to quit, when you keep "fighting the good fight of faith,"[1] by trusting and praising Me in spite of everything. Maybe that's the fight I'm calling you to now. Maybe I want to make you an example to others of faith and trust and courage and endurance and cheerfulness in the face of overwhelming odds.

You have to fight for your healing, you have to pray for endurance and not give up when the victories aren't quick and easy, but you also have to leave your life in My hands. You need patience and perseverance to stick it out and keep fighting in spirit until My purpose is accomplished, your testimony is complete, or the conditions are right for Me to help you win the victory, in whatever form that may come.

In those moments that you feel you can't take any more, hold onto Me and My promises. Let Me carry you when you don't have the strength to take another step. Let Me comfort you when there is no other comfort to be found. Let Me love you through the night, so you can greet each dawn with hope and joy and thankfulness

and faith in Me to help you fight through another day.

Whether you win a complete and final victory today or fight this battle till the day you die, either way you're a winner as long as you keep fighting. The apostle Paul didn't say at the end of his days, "I won every battle. I've defeated every enemy." He said, "I have fought the good fight, I have finished the race, I have kept the faith."[2] If you can say the same when you get to heaven, then you too will hear Me say, "Well done, good and faithful servant. Enter into the joy of your Lord!"[3]

Those words alone are worth the fight, so fight well and keep fighting till the end of whatever battle I call you to fight, short or long, temporary or terminal.

If I see fit to deliver you tomorrow, then praise Me for that. If I see fit to ask you to fight this battle again tomorrow, then praise Me for that. If I choose to let you fight this battle till your dying day, thank Me anyway and keep fighting. The trying of your faith is precious to Me. You might see yourself as a spiritual weakling, but I see the opposite—and I love what I see!

---

1. Timothy 6:12

2. Timothy 4:7

3. Matthew 25:21

CHAPTER 8

More on the Upside

String of pearls

Why does My Word say that "many are the afflictions of the righteous"?[1] Wouldn't it make more sense and be more just if I rewarded good people with good health, rather than letting them get sick? I see things differently. You think mostly in terms of the present and view problems as some sort of punishment, whereas I think in terms of lasting gains.

Consider the pearl, and you'll see what I mean. That pearl doesn't just suddenly appear in the oyster. It's the result of a process—and a painful one. It starts when a grain of sand or some other irritant makes its way into the oyster shell and the oyster reacts to the discomfort by coating the irritant in nacre, the stuff from which its own inner shell is made. This makes the "intruder" that much bigger and that much more annoying, so the oyster repeats the process over and over, forming a pearl over time—a gem from what was once just a bothersome grain of sand.

Afflictions generate the process through which some of the best qualities can be cultivated—patience, compassion, humility, kindness, gentleness, empathy, and many more. If you let them accomplish My purpose, each affliction results in a thing of beauty, a lustrous pearl. Over a lifetime, you can amass quite a few, which I string together and give back to you as a reward for all you've been through. Wear them proudly.

---

1. Psalm 34:19

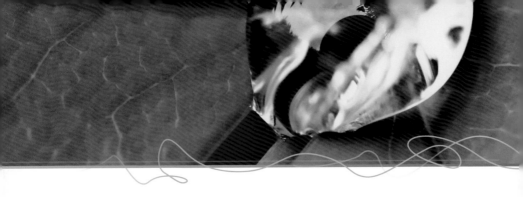

Come closer

I want to use this illness to strengthen your connection with Me as you rest in My arms and turn to My Word for encouragement. I want this to be a time of sweetness as you look to Me, like a little child looks to her father for help. I want it to be a time of soaking in My love as you let Me comfort you and nurse you back to full health.

Sometimes sickness comes as a gift of My love, to bring you to a point where you can't do anything else but lie in My arms; you can't think or move or talk or even pray. All you can do is relax and let Me comfort you and soothe you. Even though it's difficult to see My reasoning behind the pain and discomfort, I'm using it to draw you ever so close to Me, where I can whisper My love and secrets to you. I want to forge a clear channel between you and Me that will remain strong long after this illness has passed. I want to instill in you a desire to know Me better and a longing to hear My voice more clearly.

So come to Me. I'm here to hold, to comfort, and to speak to your heart. Come and rest for a while with Me, so I can give you the grace and strength and help and healing you need.

Your weakness, My strength

It pains Me to see you in pain, and I cry when you cry, but when you're weak, I remain strong.

I want to fill you with new energy—My energy, My strength, My healing. My strength and grace will always be sufficient. My arms will always be there to support you when you're weary and to lift you up when you fall. My care and protection will surround you, and I will never let the pain be greater than you and I together can bear.

When you're weak, that's a perfect chance for My strength to come through. But I can't be made strong in your weakness if you just wallow in your weakness and let it discourage you. I can only be made strong in your weakness if you'll accept what I'm doing and say, "Yes, Jesus, You win. I'm weak, I can't do it without You, so You've got to help me."

Call on Me and I will answer you. I will give to you out of My great abundance of strength and good health, so you will not lack. As long as you call on My power and let Me fight for you, you will have the strength you need. As long as you turn to Me for help, you will always have My help. So thank and praise Me for your infirmities! Glory in them, that My power may rest upon you, that in your weakness My strength may become your strength.

Let Me take your worries and fears

Times of sickness and weakness can cause worry and fear, especially as you get older. Your body is weaker, the healing process takes longer, and sometimes you're not as strong afterward. This tests your faith that I'm able to restore you to good health, even as the years pass.

At times like this, you need to remember two things: First, that no good comes from worrying, and second, that if I allow you to be weakened through sickness you can be sure that I do so in love.

The worst thing you can do is yield to the spirit of worry or fear. Worry and fear not only weaken your faith muscles, but they also weaken your physical body. Faith, on the other hand, creates and brings life and strength and energy; worry and fear tear down, faith builds up. Your greatest strength comes through faith in My love and wisdom, that I'm concerned and I know and want what's best for you.

As you spend time with Me and My Word, your faith will grow and displace those worries and fears. They may come back from time to time, but the cure is always the same—meditating on Me and My Word—and the more you do it, the stronger your resistance will become. I will keep you in perfect peace as you fix your mind on Me and My promises.

RELIEF

It hurts Me to see you suffer, especially when it goes on so long, but know this, dear one: I will not let this illness continue one moment longer than you can bear. Though your body may be pinned to the bed, your spirit can soar.

When the pain gets to be too much, set your heart and mind on things above; escape to heavenly places with Me. When boredom sets in, escape into My Word; there you will always find new truths that will thrill your spirit. When you get discouraged because you're not able to do everything you once could or would like to, count your blessings and thank Me for all I have helped you accomplish and experience in life. When you feel lonely or forgotten, reach out to someone who also needs a friend; write a letter, make a phone call, say a prayer. When being in the same sickroom day after day wears on your spirit, ask Me to give you a glimpse of heaven and the place I have prepared for you. When you feel unloved, ask Me to give you a double dose of My love. When there's no one else around and it's just you and Me, I'm nearer than I've ever been before and wait to speak fresh words of comfort and encouragement to you.

Bible Verses on Prayer

PRAISE AND THANK THE LORD BEFORE PRESENTING YOUR REQUEST TO HIM.

Let us come before His presence with thanksgiving. *Psalm 95:2*

Be anxious for nothing, but in everything by prayer and supplication, with thanksgiving, let your requests be made known to God. *Philippians 4:6*

BE SPECIFIC AND ASK FOR WHAT YOU NEED.

Ask, and it will be given to you; seek, and you will find; knock, and it will be opened to you. For everyone who asks receives, and he who seeks finds, and to him who knocks it will be opened. *Matthew 7:7–8*

Whatever things you ask in prayer, believing, you will receive. *Matthew 21:22*

PRAY IN JESUS' NAME.

If you ask anything in My name, I will do it. *John 14:14*

Whatever you ask the Father in My name He will give you. *John 16:23*

PRAYER ALSO INCLUDES LISTENING TO GOD.

It shall be, if He calls you, that you must say, "Speak, Lord, for Your servant hears." *1 Samuel 3:9*

The Lord passed by, and a great and strong wind tore into the mountains and broke the rocks in pieces before the Lord, but the Lord was not in the wind; and after the wind an earthquake, but the Lord was not in the earthquake; and after the earthquake a fire, but the Lord was not in the fire; and after the fire a still small voice. *1 Kings 19:11–12*

PRAY IN FAITH.

Being fully convinced that what He had promised He was also able to perform. *Romans 4:21*

Without faith it is impossible to please Him, for he who comes to God must believe that He is, and that He is a rewarder of those who diligently seek Him. *Hebrews 11:6*

OBEY GOD AND DO HIS WILL.

If you abide in Me, and My words abide in you, you will ask what you desire, and it shall be done for you. *John 15:7*

And whatever we ask we receive from Him, because we keep His commandments and do those things that are pleasing in His sight. *1 John 3:22*

SUBMIT YOURSELF TO GOD AND PRAY ACCORDING TO HIS WILL.

Teach me to do Your will, for You are my God; Your Spirit is good. Lead me in the land of uprightness. *Psalm 143:10*

Now this is the confidence that we have in Him, that if we ask anything according to His will, He hears us. *1 John 5:14*

PRAY HUMBLY.

We do not present our supplications before You because of our righteous deeds, but because of Your great mercies. *Daniel 9:18*

God resists the proud, but gives grace to the humble. *James 4:6*

REMIND GOD OF HIS PROMISES WHEN PRAYING.

Then Jacob said, "O God of my father Abraham and God of my father Isaac, the Lord who said to me, 'Return to your country and to your family, and I will deal well with you': I am not worthy of the least of all the mercies and of all the truth which You have shown Your servant; for I crossed over this Jordan with my staff, and now I have become two companies. Deliver me, I pray, from the hand of my brother, from the hand of Esau; for I fear him, lest he come and attack me and the mother with the children. For You said, 'I will surely treat you well, and make your descendants as the sand of the sea, which cannot be numbered for multitude.'" *Genesis 32:9–12*

Bible Verses on Healing

GOD CAN HEAL.

Who forgives all your iniquities, who heals all your diseases. *Psalm 103:3*

"For I will restore health to you and heal you of your wounds," says the Lord. *Jeremiah 30:17*

To you who fear My name the Sun of Righteousness shall arise with healing in His wings. *Malachi 4:2*

GOD WANTS TO HEAL.

For He does not afflict willingly, Nor grieve the children of men. *Lamentations 3:33*

Therefore strengthen the hands which hang down, and the feeble knees, and make straight paths for your feet, so that what is lame may not be dislocated, but rather be healed. *Hebrews 12:12–13*

NOTHING IS TOO SERIOUS FOR GOD TO HEAL.

Behold, I am the Lord, the God of all flesh. Is there anything too hard for Me? *Jeremiah 32:27*

If you can believe, all things are possible to him who believes. *Mark 9:23*

HEALING WAS PART OF JESUS' EARTHLY MINISTRY.

Jesus went about all Galilee, teaching in their synagogues, preaching the gospel of the kingdom, and healing all kinds of sickness and all kinds of disease among the people. They brought to Him all sick people who were afflicted with various diseases and torments, and those who were demon-possessed, epileptics, and paralytics; and He healed them. *Matthew 4:23–24*

Great multitudes followed Him, and He healed them all. *Matthew 12:15*

JESUS' HEALING POWER IS STILL AT WORK TODAY.

And these signs will follow those who believe: In My name they will cast out demons; they will speak with new tongues; they will take up serpents; and if they drink anything deadly, it will by no means hurt them; they will lay hands on the sick, and they will recover. *Mark 16:17–18*

Jesus Christ is the same yesterday, today, and forever. *Hebrews 13:8*

Eight Steps to Healing and Other Miracles

1. Begin with a clean heart; unconfessed sin in your life will hinder faith.

He who covers his sins will not prosper, but whoever confesses and forsakes them will have mercy. *Proverbs 28:13*

If our heart does not condemn us, we have confidence toward God. *1 John 3:21*

2. Prepare by memorizing promises; find authority in God's Word and faith will follow.

Faith comes by hearing, and hearing by the word of God. *Romans 10:17*

Not one thing has failed of all the good things which the Lord your God spoke concerning you. All have come to pass for you; not one word of them has failed. *Joshua 23:14*

Heaven and earth will pass away, but My words will by no means pass away. *Matthew 24:35*

3. Be definite.

Concerning the work of My hands, you command Me. *Isaiah 45:11*

Ask, and you will receive, that your joy may be full. *John 16:24*

4. Expect from God; know you are entitled to His promises.

Whatever things you ask when you pray, believe that you receive them, and you will have them. *Mark 11:24*

Let us therefore come boldly to the throne of grace, that we may obtain mercy and find grace to help in time of need. *Hebrews 4:16*

5. Accept from God; there comes a time to cease praying.

So the Lord said to Joshua: "Get up! Why do you lie thus on your face?" *Joshua 7:10*

Mary said, "Behold the maidservant of the Lord! Let it be to me according to your word." *Luke 1:38*

6. Stand your ground in faith and trust, even if you don't see the answer immediately.

God is not a man, that He should lie … Has He said, and will He not do? Or has He spoken, and will He not make it good? *Numbers 23:19*

"I believe God that it will be just as it was told me." *Acts 27:25*

Therefore do not cast away your confidence, which has great reward. For you have need of endurance, so that after you have done the will of God, you may receive the promise. *Hebrews 10:35–36*

That the genuineness of your faith, being much more precious than gold that perishes, though it is tested by fire, may be found to praise, honor, and glory at the revelation of Jesus Christ. *1 Peter 1:7*

7. PUT YOUR FAITH INTO ACTION.

[Jesus] entered the synagogue again, and a man was there who had a withered hand. … He said to the man, "Stretch out your hand." And he stretched it out, and his hand was restored as whole as the other. *Mark 3:1,5*

There was a certain nobleman whose son was sick at Capernaum. He went to [Jesus] and implored Him to come down and heal his son, for he was at the point of death. … Jesus said to him, "Go your way; your son lives." So the man believed the word that Jesus spoke to him, and he went his way. And as he was now going down, his servants met him and told him, saying, "Your son lives!" Then he inquired of them the hour when he got better. And they said to him, "Yesterday at the seventh hour the fever left him." So the father knew that it was at the same hour in which Jesus said to him, "Your son lives." And he himself believed, and his whole household. *John 4:46–53*

8. THANK HIM FOR HEARING AND ANSWERING YOUR PRAYER.

You have turned for me my mourning into dancing; You have put off my sackcloth and clothed me with gladness, to the end that my glory may sing praise to You and not be silent. O Lord my God, I will give thanks to You forever. *Psalm 30:11–12*

Let the redeemed of the Lord say so, whom He has redeemed from the hand of the enemy. *Psalm 107:2*

Healing is for You

COMPILED FROM THE WRITINGS OF **D. B. BERG**

The day of miracles is not past! God is still alive, well, and working just as powerfully as ever amongst those who trust in Him. He says, "I am the Lord, I change not,"[1] and Jesus Christ is "the same yesterday, today and forever."[2]

To heal is a small thing for the God of all creation. If He created the body, He can certainly fix it! He says, "I am the Lord, the God of all flesh. Is there anything too hard for Me?"[3]

This is only one of many promises of healing that can be found in the Bible—promises that you can claim as your own and expect Him to fulfill. This is also where your faith for His supernatural healing will come from. Faith comes, it grows, by hearing the Word of God.[4] Faith is built on the Word, so read it prayerfully and ask God to strengthen your faith.

God not only *can* heal you, but He *wants* to heal you. A leper once came to Jesus and said, "Lord, if You are willing, You can make me clean." Jesus touched the man and said, "I am willing; be cleansed," and immediately the man's leprosy was cleansed.[5] He's more willing to give than we are to receive. All He asks is that we honor Him with faith by believing His promises.

Prayer power!

"The prayer of faith will save the sick, and the Lord will raise him up."[6] Prayer is powerful. When we pray, things will happen and things will be different. He promises, "If you ask anything in My name, I will do it,"[7] and "No good thing will He withhold from those who walk uprightly."[8] You've got these and all of the other promises in the Bible on your side—"exceeding great and precious promises"[9]—so when you pray for healing or anything else, bring those promises with you to remind God of His Word. Doing so is a positive declaration of your faith, which pleases Him.

You usually don't see the blessing—His healing, in this case—the instant you begin praying for it. You have His promises in His Word, but how do you know He's going to keep them? You've got to *prove* Him. You've got to put those promises to the test. You've got to challenge God. He even tells us, "Concerning the work of My hands, you command Me."[10] So hold Him to His Word. *Expect* an answer. He has promised it. Put your faith in the Lord, and claim scriptures. He is bound by His Word, so remind Him of His promises, cling to them, and never doubt for a moment that He is going to answer—and He will. He has to! He wants to! Trust Him!

Jesus says, "Whatever things you ask when you pray, believe that you receive them, and you will have them."[11] "Now this is the confidence that we have in Him, that if we ask anything according to His will, He hears us. And if we know that He hears us, whatever we ask, we know that we have the petitions that we have asked of Him."[12] All we have to do is believe His promises, pray, and expect Him to answer.

1. Malachi 3:6
2. Hebrews 13:8
3. Jeremiah 32:27
4. Romans 10:17
5. Matthew 8:2–3
6. James 5:15
7. John 14:14
8. Psalm 84:11
9. 2 Peter 1:4
10. Isaiah 45:11
11. Mark 11:24
12. 1 John 5:14–15

The "test of faith"

One of the greatest of healing factors is faith—knowing that God loves us and is concerned about our health and happiness, and that He is going to take care of us no matter what. But He often tests our faith before He heals us, because He wants to see if we'll believe His promises and continue to love and trust Him even if we think we may never get healed. Before He honors us with healing, He wants to see if we will honor Him with faith.

Ongoing illnesses are sometimes a severe test, and sad to say, they sometimes end in bitterness, complaining, and even holding a grievance against God because He doesn't heal the way the person wants Him to or thinks He should. "God doesn't love me, He doesn't care, because He won't heal me!" That sort of reaction is the opposite of faith, and "without faith it is impossible to please Him, for he who comes to God must believe that He is, and that He is a rewarder of those who diligently seek Him."[13]

God can and wants to heal us, but we must first make the decision that we want what *He* wants and knows is best for us, without reservations. We must also do our part by first correcting any physical or spiritual problems that may be contributing factors. Then you can pray and trust God for your healing, and you're bound to get results!

---

13. Hebrews 11:6

A Prayer for Healing

Below is a sample prayer for healing, based on the principles described in this book. This prayer also presumes that the one praying has received Jesus' gift of salvation (see page 68). You may want to use it as is, or pray something like it tailored to your own need and request.

Jesus, I thank You for the privilege of knowing You. Thank You for how You came into my life, and blessed me with the gift of eternal life and a place in heaven. You gave Your life for me because You love me, and I can't thank You enough for that.

I thank You for also allowing Your body to be broken as You suffered and died. "By Your stripes we are healed,"[1] and I can now benefit from the priceless gift of physical healing in addition to spiritual healing. I truly appreciate both the sacrifice You made long ago, and the healing power that You make available to us today.

When You walked the earth, You did miracles, including healing diseases, and the Bible states clearly that You are "the same yesterday, today, and forever."[2] That means that You have the power to heal me now, when I'm weak and sick and in need. I ask You humbly for the gift of Your healing touch. Please take this affliction away, in Your time and in the way You know is best.

---

1. Isaiah 53:5

2. Hebrews 13:8

If there is anything in my life that I need to make right in order to receive Your healing, please show me. I am willing to make changes and improvements, to more closely align my life with Your standards.

I ask for this healing not only for myself, but also so that I can have the health and strength to in turn give to and care for others who need me. I want to testify to them of Your love and of Your power to heal.

I believe Your words that say that "whatever things we ask in prayer, believing, we will receive."[3] I believe in Your power and in the power of prayer. I expect that in answer to this prayer, I will see change, progress, and healing. I thank You for it! Amen.

---

3. Matthew 21:22

Afterword

If you haven't yet experienced the kind of love expressed in these messages from Jesus, it may be that you haven't yet received His gifts of eternal love and life by accepting Him as your Savior. Jesus waits humbly for you to invite Him into your life. He says, "Behold, I stand at the door [of your heart] and knock. If anyone hears My voice and opens the door, I will come in."[1] You can receive Him right now by sincerely praying the following:

Dear Jesus, thank You for dying for me so I can have eternal life. Please forgive me for every wrong and unloving thing I have ever done. Wash away all that, and help me to do better. I need Your love to fill and satisfy my heart. I want the life of happiness You have for me—here and now, and in heaven hereafter. I open the door of my heart and ask You, Jesus, to come in. Thank You for hearing and answering my prayer, and thank You for helping me share Your love and be a force for good in the lives of others. Amen.

---

1. Revelation 3:20